Lerner SPORTS

ALL-STAR SMACKDOWN

SOPHIA SMITH VS. ABBY WAMBACH

WHO WOULD WIN?

ANNE E. HILL

Lerner Publications ◆ Minneapolis

Lerner Publications Company
An imprint of Lerner Publishing Group, Inc.
241 First Avenue North
Minneapolis, MN 55401 USA

For reading levels and more information, look up this title at www.lernerbooks.com.

Main body text set in Aptifer Sans LT Pro.
Typeface provided by Linotype AG.

Editor: Nicole Berglund **Photo Editor:** Nicole Berglund

Library of Congress Cataloging-in-Publication Data

Names: Hill, Anne E., 1974– author.
Title: Sophia Smith vs. Abby Wambach : who would win? / Anne E. Hill.
Other titles: Sophia Smith versus Abby Wambach
Description: Minneapolis : Lerner Publications, [2025] | Series: Lerner sports. All-star smackdown | Includes bibliographical references and index. | Audience: Ages 7–11 years | Audience: Grades 2–3 | Summary: "Born 20 years apart, Sophia Smith and Abby Wambach have both ruled the soccer field as forwards. But who is better? Readers will compare their careers side by side, and choose a winner"— Provided by publisher.
Identifiers: LCCN 2024008806 (print) | LCCN 2024008807 (ebook) | ISBN 9798765648278 (lib. bdg.) | ISBN 9798765661437 (pbk.) | ISBN 9798765653272 (epub)
Subjects: LCSH: Soccer for women—United States—Juvenile literature. | Women soccer players—Rating of—United States—Juvenile literature. | Smith, Sophia—Juvenile literature. | Wambach, Abby, 1980-—Juvenile literature. | Sports rivalries—United States—History—Juvenile literature.
Classification: LCC GV944.5 .H55 2025 (print) | LCC GV944.5 (ebook) | DDC 796.334092/520973—dc23/eng/20240403

LC record available at https://lccn.loc.gov/2024008806
LC ebook record available at https://lccn.loc.gov/2024008807

Manufactured in the United States of America
1-1010830-53385-7/23/2024

TABLE OF CONTENTS

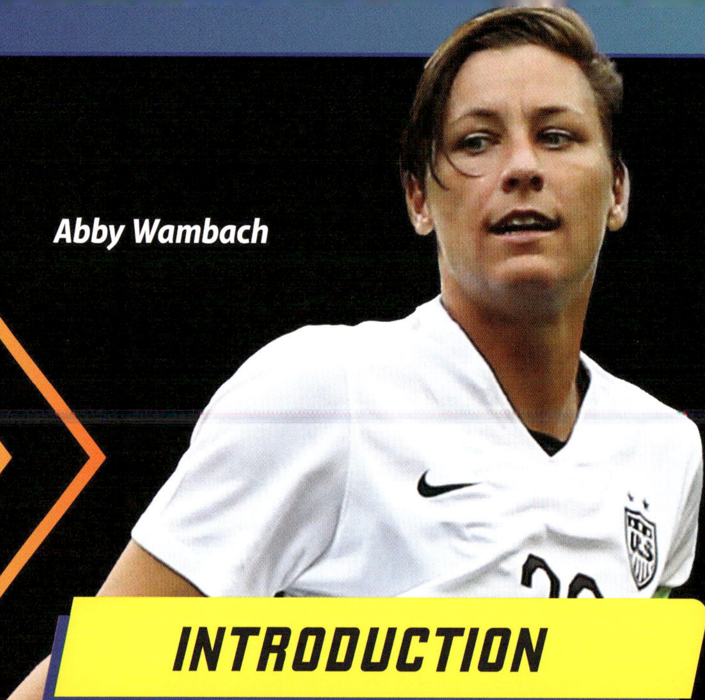

Abby Wambach

INTRODUCTION

GOING FOR IT

In 2015, US soccer player Abby Wambach appeared in her fourth and final FIFA World Cup. The 35-year-old had announced her retirement just before the tournament. She was proud of her bronze and silver Women's World Cup medals, but she was missing a gold.

Fast Facts

- Abby Wambach played pro soccer from 2001–2015.
- Wambach is a member of the National Soccer Hall of Fame.
- Sophia Smith competed for the US on the Under-17 (U-17), Under-20 (U-20), and senior national teams.
- Smith was the first player born in the 2000s to play for the women's senior national team.

The tournament was hard-fought, and Wambach helped advance her team to the final against Japan.

The stadium in Vancouver, Canada, was buzzing on July 5, 2015. More than 50,000 soccer fans packed the stands. Carli Lloyd scored a hat trick for the US team, but Japan answered with two goals. The minutes ticked down with Team USA leading 5–2. They did not ease up. Wambach entered the game in its 79th minute. Soon she helped lift the World Cup trophy! She finally had the gold to end her amazing career as a forward.

Sophia Smith

Sophia Smith is another high-scoring forward for Team USA. In 2023, she was in Australia and New Zealand, playing in her first FIFA World Cup. Smith scored a brace and had an assist in the first match of the tournament. Her efforts helped her team win 3–0 over Vietnam.

Team USA didn't win the World Cup in 2023. But Smith had proved herself on the international soccer stage. She hasn't won a World Cup yet, but she has plenty of amazing plays ahead of her. Will she become as successful as her idol Abby Wambach? Who will win this smackdown? Read on to find out!

Smith controls the ball during the 2023 FIFA Women's World Cup.

Wambach plays in the US team's final game before the 2015 FIFA Women's World Cup.

CHAPTER 1

Wambach plays for the Washington Freedom in 2003.

BORN TO PLAY

Abby Wambach and Sophia Smith both come from athletic families that love sports. Wambach was born on June 2, 1980, in Rochester, New York. She has four older brothers and two older sisters. She learned to compete and play sports with them. This made her very tough to beat. She played soccer and basketball in high school. But Wambach gave up basketball to concentrate on her love for soccer.

Her skills and strong play led her to the High School All-America team as well as the Olympic Development Program. She achieved all this before she started college! In 1998, Wambach started attending the University of Florida. The Florida Gators won the Southeastern Conference championships all four years Wambach played with the team. She made a record-shattering 96 goals in her college career.

Wambach (right) hits the ball with her head in a 2003 game.

It was no surprise when she was selected in the first round of the 2002 Women's United Soccer Association draft by the Washington Freedom.

Wambach in a 2002 game for the Washington Freedom

Smith plays for Stanford University in 2019.

Sophia Smith was born on August 10, 2000, in Windsor, Colorado. She is the youngest of three daughters. Her sisters and father all played basketball. Like Wambach, Smith played both soccer and basketball in high school. But soccer soon won out.

Smith kicks the ball in a 2019 game with Stanford.

CONSIDER THIS

Wambach and Smith have both appeared in TV and print ads. They have endorsed products for many companies. Both work with the sporting goods company Nike to empower young women to play soccer.

Smith went on to play at Stanford University for two years. At Stanford, Smith led the team to a national title. She decided to leave college in 2019 to play pro soccer. Fans were excited when she was selected by the Portland Thorns as the number one pick in the 2020 National Women's Soccer League (NWSL) draft.

Smith holds up a Portland Thorns scarf at the 2020 NWSL draft.

CHAPTER 2

Wambach (right) hits the ball with her head during a match at the 2011 FIFA Women's World Cup.

TOP OF THEIR GAMES

Wambach and Smith were both standout young athletes who became pro soccer players after college. As starting forwards, their main job is to score goals. But Wambach and Smith have different styles of play that have led to their successes.

Wambach is 5 feet 11 (1.8 m). Her height and aggressive playing helped her succeed. As a young player, Wambach would stay late after practice to work on headers. Headers involve a player hitting the soccer ball with their head. They can be very dangerous and often lead to injuries. Wambach tried to perfect her diving header, a skill that became her signature play. Though it is dangerous, it has helped her win many games.

Wambach hits a header at a 2015 game.

Wambach (right) heads the ball during a 2011 FIFA Women's World Cup game.

At the 2011 World Cup with a US victory on the line, Wambach performed one of the greatest headers in women's pro soccer. In a game against Brazil, the US team was a goal behind in the last minutes of regular play. Teammate Megan

Rapinoe took the ball toward the Brazilian goal. She fired it high to Wambach, who headed it into the goal to tie the game!

The US went on to win the game in a shoot-out. Then they beat France before losing to Japan in the final. The amazing goal against Brazil earned Wambach ESPN's 2011 Best Game ESPY Award. Her efforts won her the FIFA Silver Ball award in addition to her silver-medal finish at that year's Cup. The Silver Ball award goes to the second-best player in the World Cup.

Wambach (left) holds her Silver Ball award after the 2011 FIFA Women's World Cup.

Sophia Smith has her own style of play centered on her incredible speed and quick moves. In 2020, she became the first player born in the 2000s to compete for the US senior national team. She had already competed on the U-17 and U-20 national teams.

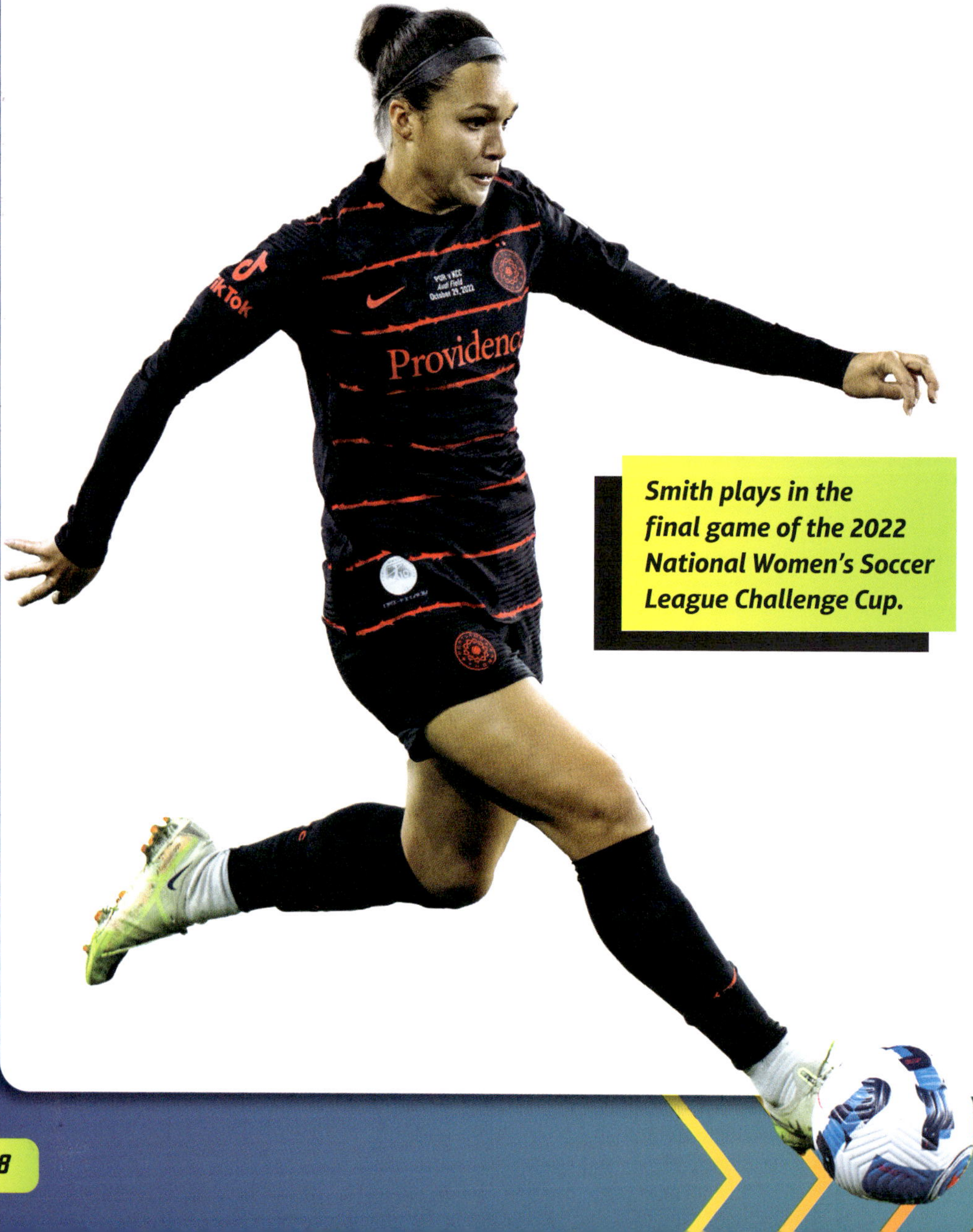

Smith plays in the final game of the 2022 National Women's Soccer League Challenge Cup.

CONSIDER THIS

Smith considers Wambach her soccer idol. Wambach has shared praise for Smith online. The two even met when Smith was a little girl! Smith waited in a long line of fans to meet Wambach after a game.

Smith (center) plays for the Portland Thorns in 2022.

Smith was an important player for the Portland Thorns. In April 2023, she scored her first pro hat trick against the Kansas City Current. She was the league's top scorer that year. Many consider Smith to be one of the brightest stars in the future of women's soccer.

CHAPTER 3

Wambach (center) celebrates her team's gold medal win at the 2012 Olympic Games.

LEGENDS ON THE FIELD

Wambach has played in four World Cups, earning a total medal haul of two bronze, one silver, and one gold. She has also played in two Olympics, taking home two gold medals. In her last Olympic Games in London, England, in 2012, Wambach scored in every match except the final. Her opening-round header was the first US goal of the Games. Later, Team USA won the final against Japan and earned the gold medal.

Wambach was named the 2012 FIFA Women's World Player of the Year. She added this award to the many others she received during her career. She is a six-time winner of the US Soccer Female Player of the Year award. She had a record-setting 184 international goals scored. Until Canadian player Christine Sinclair passed Wambach in 2020, no male or female player had beaten her record.

Wambach celebrates a goal during the 2012 Olympic Games.

Smith (right) controls the ball during a 2019 Stanford game.

In 2020, Smith was just beginning her career as a senior for the US Women's National Team. She had already helped the Stanford Cardinal to two college championships. She was also the first pick of the NWSL draft by the Portland Thorns. An injury cut her first pro season short.

In 2021, Smith scored seven goals and helped her team advance to the playoffs. Her 2022 season was even more impressive. Smith was named MVP for the season as well as the final match, which the Thorns won. In her 2023 season, Smith was the league's top scorer.

CONSIDER THIS

July 20 is Abby Wambach Day! In 2011, the mayor of Rochester, Abby's hometown, declared the day to honor the soccer star. She received a key to the city. After her 2012 Olympic win, the entrance of Sahlen's Stadium in Rochester was named Wambach Way.

Smith** (center right) **plays against Sweden in the 2023 FIFA Women's World Cup.

After the US women lost in the 2023 World Cup, Smith helped the team win gold in the 2024 Olympics in Paris, France. She also plans to play a big role on the next World Cup team in 2027.

CHAPTER 4

Wambach plays for the US Women's National Team in 2015.

AND THE WINNER IS

Who is the better starting forward in this soccer smackdown? You get to decide! Everyone has different opinions, and that's okay. It's part of the fun of being a sports fan. So who do you think is better?

On September 21, 2019, Abby Wambach became a member of the National Soccer Hall of Fame. Just a few months later, Sophia Smith was called up to the US senior national team. She continues to play and hopes to have a long career like her idol, Wambach.

Smith plays for the US Women's National Team in 2021.

Smith holds her trophy for 2022 US Soccer Female Player of the Year.

Wambach and Smith are both considered superstars in women's soccer. Smith still has many big games to play. But for now, the winner is Abby Wambach. Her stats, awards, and Hall of Fame status are hard to beat. Smith has had an amazing start to her pro career. She hopes to win as many medals and awards as Wambach did. And Smith may do just that. Do you think she can beat Wambach's numbers someday?

Wambach gives a speech at the National Soccer Hall of Fame in 2019.

SMACKDOWN BREAKDOWN

ABBY WAMBACH

Date of birth: June 2, 1980
Height: 5 feet 11 (1.8 m)
FIFA Women's World Cup wins: 1
Olympic medals: 2
International goals scored: 184

Stats are accurate through the 2023 season.

SOPHIA SMITH

Date of birth: August 10, 2000
Height: 5 feet 6 (1.7 m)
FIFA Women's World Cup wins: 0
Olympic medals: 1
International goals scored: 23

GLOSSARY

assist: a pass that leads to a goal

brace: when a player scores two goals in one game

FIFA: a group that oversees soccer around the world

final: the championship match of a tournament

forward: a player whose main role is to score goals

hat trick: when a player scores three goals in one game

header: using your head to hit a soccer ball

idol: a greatly loved and admired person or thing

MVP: most valuable player

shoot-out: a way to break a tied game by having players shoot directly at the opponents' goalie

signature play: a play that an athlete uses often

LEARN MORE

Flynn, Brendan. *Girls' Soccer.* Minneapolis: SportsZone, 2022.

Goldstein, Margaret J. *Meet Sophia Smith: US Soccer Superstar.* Minneapolis: Lerner Publications, 2024.

Kiddle: FIFA World Cup Facts for Kids
https://kids.kiddle.co/FIFA_World_Cup

Lowe, Alexander. *G.O.A.T. Soccer Strikers.* Minneapolis: Lerner Publications, 2022.

Sports Illustrated Kids: Abby Wambach Breaks Mia Hamm's Scoring Record
https://www.sikids.com/goalazo/abby-wambach-breaks-mia-hamms-scoring-record

US Soccer: Sophia Smith
https://www.ussoccer.com/players/s/sophia-smith

INDEX

PHOTO ACKNOWLEDGMENTS

Image credits: AP Photo/Icon Sportswire, pp. 4, 7; AP Photo/Kim Price/Cal Sport Media, pp. 5, 29; AP Photo/Jose Breton/Pics Action/NurPhoto, p. 6; Jeff Gross/Getty Images, p. 8; tony quinn/Alamy, p. 9; Craig Jones/Getty Images, p. 10; John Todd/ISI Photos/Getty Images, pp. 11–12, 22; Jose L. Argueta/ISI Photos/Getty Images, p. 13; AP Photo/Marcio Jose Sanchez, p. 14; AP Photo/TFV Media, p. 15; Jonathan Larsen/Diadem Images/Alamy, p. 16; Christof Koepsel/Getty Images, p. 17; Brad Smith/ISI Photos/Getty Images, p. 18; AP Photo/Dantey Buitureida/SPP/Sipa USA, p. 19; Ronald Martinez/Getty Images, pp. 20, 27; AP Photo/Ben Curtis, p. 21; UK Sports Pics Ltd/Alamy, p. 23; AP Photo/Stephen Lew/Cal Sport Media, p. 24; Omar Vega/Getty Images, p. 25; AP Photo/Nick Wass, p. 26; Chris Covatta/Stringer/Getty Images, p. 28.

Cover: AP Photo/Cal Sport Media; tony quinn/Alamy.